Table of Contents

Dave and Wanda

I sat on their living room floor, "weeping with those who weep," (Romans 12:15). Feelings of unthinkable pain and loss hung heavy in the room. The officer explained what happened. Their granddaughter had been brutally murdered by three men. She was twenty-one. Grief gripped this family for weeks. Dave and Wanda are committed followers of Christ, practicing the three experiences contained in this Impact Guide every day. Though hurting terribly, they pressed into God. They asked God to sustain them with His truth and promises. They requested adjustments and assignments from the Holy Spirit. They bade God bring the support and encouragement into their lives to carry them through this pain. God heard their cries. Support poured in. A clear assignment from the Holy Spirit came. An unexplainable sense of peace and purpose began to flow into their hearts. They sensed that the Lord wanted them to give the message of His grace and love, the gospel of forgiveness and eternal life, to the three men that brutally murdered their granddaughter. It didn't make sense. It wasn't natural. It was supernatural.

The day came for the family to address the perpetrators of this horror in court. Dave spoke with confidence and compassion, explaining the love of God in Christ for these men. When he recounted it to me, he said he had never felt so carried along and directed by the Holy Spirit. The men broke and wept as Dave shared God's love in Christ. The officers broke and wept. Christ was magnified in a court of law as the light of hope pierced the darkness.

Glenn

"Man, something is happening in me right now! I don't know how to explain it." These were the words of Mark, Glenn's friend, just before he embraced

Christ as his Savior. Glenn is a middle-aged, single man. He loves the Lord and is seeking the adjustments and assignments of the Holy Spirit. One day, he sensed a need to reconnect with Mark, a childhood friend. He invited him over for Thanksgiving dinner. During the conversation, he shared the difference Christ had made in his own life. Glenn guided his friend toward opening his heart to Christ. Mark made the decision to receive Jesus and asked if Glenn could help him get baptized. Glenn called me and together, we baptized Mark the following Sunday morning.

Two weeks later Mark received an assignment from the Holy Spirit to reach out to his son Tristan. Tristan is a young man getting ready to enter Marine boot camp. Mark shared his experience with his son. Tristan's response was, "Dad, I've always known that I need God in my life but no one has ever shared about receiving Jesus and believing what he accomplished." Tristan told his dad that he wanted to receive Jesus and he did! They contacted me and the following week, Tristan professed his faith publicly through believer's baptism.

Glenn was baptized and has learned to be in the Word, yielding to the Spirit's assignments leading to Mark coming to Christ and being baptized leading to Tristan coming to Christ and being baptized. This is the movement of the Holy Spirit.

The Chicken Coop

Larry sat with me at the table on the front porch of our cabin. He asked me to give him direction and assignments to serve God. I told him that giving spiritual assignments is the job of the Holy Spirit and our job as spiritual friends is to support and encourage people when they get direction from the

Lord. He seemed frustrated. I explained that a follower of Christ should have a conversation with God every day seeking three things: truth and promises, adjustments and assignments, support and encouragement. I said the conversation with God should go something like this:

Father, as I read or listen to your Word, I ask you to open my eyes to the truth in it that sets me free (John 8:32) and the promises that empower me (2 Peter 1:4). Then read or listen, writing down anything the Father reveals to you.

Secondly, tell the Holy Spirit that you are yielding to Him (Galatians 5:16).

Holy Spirit, I yield my life to you and ask you to reveal any adjustments or assignments you have for me today. Jesus taught, in John 16:14, that the Holy Spirit would always magnify Him. So, every adjustment and assignment from the Holy Spirit will make Christ known to others. Holy Spirit assignments usually have names.

Thirdly, support and encouragement should be shared with other believers (Romans 12:15)

Lord, open my eyes to the support and encouragement I need to give, and bring encouragement and support into my life today.

Larry started having this daily conversation with God. One day as I was visiting him at his house, I asked him if he had received any adjustments or assignments from the Holy Spirit. He asked me to follow him out behind the house. There was an overgrown, sheet-metal shack, full of...let's just say...animal organics. Larry said, "I sensed the Holy Spirit telling me that this is supposed to be ministry space." I cocked my head sideways and squinted my eyes at first. Then I said a silent prayer, "Holy Spirit, do you have anything you want me to say to Larry right now?" Immediately the words 'create and cultivate' came to mind. I said, "Larry, I think God just told me to tell you 'create and cultivate'." And he did! That sheet-metal shack became the Ministry Barn. It is a wonderful, rustic building that facilitates discipleship for men, women, and a food and clothing ministry for the community. People are coming to the Lord, deepening their walk with God, and impacting the community by meeting needs. This is an example of Impact Multiplied (the name of our ministry movement).

Men's Group meeting at the Ministry Barn

Im•pact – *noun /im pakt/* - strong influence, collision, moving someone to action.

"Don't just listen to God's word. Do what it says. Otherwise, you are only fooling yourselves." James 1:22

Have you ever been 'moved to action' by the truth of God's Word? Have you gotten specific assignments from the Holy Spirit to show God's love or share Christ with someone? God wants that for you! Jesus came so that we could have a daily, dynamic relationship with God that impacts the world, expresses His love, and extends His kingdom. This is not supposed to be the experience of the ordained or hyper-spiritual. God wants it to be the daily experience of ordinary believers. Kingdom impact happens when ordinary people listen to God.

*"The members of the council were amazed when they saw the boldness of Peter and John, for they could see that they were **ordinary men** with no special training in the Scriptures. They also recognized them as men who had been with Jesus."*

Acts 4:13

Three Essential Experiences (E3)

First Experience: Getting *Truth and Promises*

Jesus said, "...*you will know the truth, and the truth will set you free."*

John 8:32

A **truth** is an instruction from the Lord designed to guide our thoughts and behavior. They are principles to avoid pitfalls. Have you ever found yourself in a low spot wondering, "How did I ever get here?" Living in God's truth helps us avoid those places and break free from chains that bind or blind us.

The **promises** of God are treasures that belongs to all who receive Christ (2 Corinthians 1:20). They empower us to overcome corrupt human desires. 7,487 verses in the Bible contain promises from God to believers. These promises are blessings of God's grace, empowering us to be overcomers in Christ.

"And because of his glory and excellence, he has given us great and precious promises. These are the promises that enable you to share his divine nature and escape the world's corruption caused by human desires."

2 Peter 1:4

Second Experience: Getting *Adjustments and Assignments*

Jesus made a promise to His followers. He said, "I will not leave you alone" (John 14:18). He told them that if He went away, the Holy Spirit would come to them and live in them! Who is this Holy Spirit? He is God in us, our counselor, comforter, guide and teacher. He is our constant companion. His goal is to magnify Christ through our lives (John 16:14). This means He wants more of the character and actions of Christ to shine out in our day-to-day life. Each day He wants to adjust some things IN US and assign some things TO US for this to happen. It's as if He says, "We are going to need to work on 'X' together so Christ can shine more brightly through you." That is the adjustment. The assignment is always an action that impacts *people*. Sometimes the Holy Spirit makes an assignment clear during your devotion time. Other times assignments come during the day and you are sensitive to them *because* you've spent time with God. The important thing to remember is that *the Holy Spirit works by invitation.* "So I say, allow the Holy Spirit guide your lives..." (Galatians 5:16a). We must invite the Holy Spirit to make His adjustments and give His assignments. If we sincerely want this, we'll experience His magnificent work. He is God and He always blesses His own work (Ephesians 3:20)! That's why a heartfelt request like, "Holy Spirit, please make me sensitive to any assignments you have for me throughout this day," is so vital.

Third Experience: Sharing *Support and Encouragement*
The Bible clearly teaches that we need to give and receive support and
encouragement (Romans 12:15). The Bible teaches that the world is
"at enmity with God" (Romans 8:7). This means the world is opposed
to God's ways. Therefore, it is a challenge to live for God's glory. We
need help every day as we strive to live by the truth and promises of
God's Word and seek to live out the adjustments and assignments
given to us by the Holy Spirit.

*"Let us think of ways to motivate one another to acts of love and good
works. And let us not neglect our meeting together, as some people do,
but encourage one another, especially now that the day of his return is
drawing near."*   Hebrews 10:24-25

Making it a Conversation with God

Your relationship with God grows like any other relationship, through
good communication.

1. Father, as I look into your word today, will you open my eyes
    and understanding to grasp the truth and promises that you
    have for me today.
2. Holy Spirit, I am asking you to make me sensitive to the
    adjustments and assignments you have for me.
3. Lord, I am asking for all the support and encouragement I need
    to act on what you show me. Also, will you guide me to give the
    support and encouragement to other believers trying to live for
    you.

Once you have had your devotion time and have made some notes in
each section, turn that insight into a prayer of gratitude and request
God's guidance in it. Take some time to lift other's needs before God
and lastly your own needs and desires.

Using the '345 My Time' process with the Impact Guide

345 stands for three-minutes and forty-five seconds, the length of time it takes to listen to the average chapter of an audio Bible. There are 260 chapters in the New Testament. Five chapters per week takes you through the New Testament each year. The 345 My Time process is included at the end of this Impact Guide, but can also be found online at www.345mytime.com or any website connected with the Impact Multiplied movement. On the website, simply click on the chapter and you can read or listen. Use the Guide to record the three experiences of discipleship: Truth and Promises, Adjustments and Assignments, and Support and Encouragement.

Your Impact Log

Today's Chapter: **Date:**

Truth and Promises:
Father, what are the truths and promises you have for me today?

_____

_____

_____

_____

_____

Adjustments and Assignments:
Holy Spirit, what adjustments and assignments do you have for me today?

_____

_____

_____

_____

Support and Encouragement
What support or encouragement do I need to share or experience today?

_____

_____

_____

_____

Prayer
You can turn these experiences into a prayer here or record prayer needs you are lifting to God.

_____

_____

_____

_____

Your Impact Log

Today's Chapter: **Date:**

Truth and Promises:
Father, what are the truths and promises you have for me today?

_____

_____

_____

_____

Adjustments and Assignments:
Holy Spirit, what adjustments and assignments do you have for me today?

_____

_____

_____

Support and Encouragement
What support or encouragement do I need to share or experience today?

_____

_____

_____

Prayer
You can turn these experiences into a prayer here or record prayer needs you are lifting to God.

_____

_____

_____

Your Impact Log

Today's Chapter: **Date:**

Truth and Promises:
Father, what are the truths and promises you have for me today?

_____

_____

_____

_____

_____

Adjustments and Assignments:
Holy Spirit, what adjustments and assignments do you have for me today?

_____

_____

_____

Support and Encouragement
What support or encouragement do I need to share or experience today?

_____

_____

_____

Prayer
You can turn these experiences into a prayer here or record prayer needs you are lifting to God.

_____

_____

_____

Your Impact Log

Today's Chapter: **Date:**

Truth and Promises:

Father, what are the truths and promises you have for me today?

_____

_____

_____

_____

_____

Adjustments and Assignments:

Holy Spirit, what adjustments and assignments do you have for me today?

_____

_____

_____

Support and Encouragement

What support or encouragement do I need to share or experience today?

_____

_____

_____

Prayer

You can turn these experiences into a prayer here or record prayer needs you are lifting to God.

_____

_____

_____

Your Impact Log

Today's Chapter: **Date:**

Truth and Promises:

Father, what are the truths and promises you have for me today?

_____

_____

_____

_____

_____

Adjustments and Assignments:

Holy Spirit, what adjustments and assignments do you have for me today?

_____

_____

_____

Support and Encouragement

What support or encouragement do I need to share or experience today?

_____

_____

_____

Prayer

You can turn these experiences into a prayer here or record prayer needs you are lifting to God.

_____

_____

_____

_____

Impact Point

The path of Christ is not a religious system. Religious systems are man-made attempts to categorize everything into two classifications: things *required* and things *forbidden*. People who make Christianity just another system will laser-focus on *do's and don'ts*. They establish rules to fit their system. New ones will be added as they see fit.

A person on the path with Christ begins as a *Seeker*. Something causes this person to seek God. These causes have been described as '*seasons of the soul*.' Often the Seeker must overcome negative religious experiences to embrace a meaningful relationship with a loving God.

One Seeker was exposed to church as a child, but sporadically. A friend invited him to attend his church on a Sunday evening. It was a big step for a teenager, going to an unfamiliar place to hear a message about God. As he walked through the church door, a man who was supposed to be greeting people, was instead 'policing' people. He asked what kind of Bible he was carrying. It was a Bible given as a gift from a very kind, older lady whose family was known for serving his community with compassion. The greeter snatched the Bible from his hand and said, "You can't carry that into this place. It's not the right version!" He shoved a hardback copy of their church's required version into the teenager's hand and announced that he was now qualified to enter. The young man never got his cherished Bible back. That man, and that church, followed a system, not the Savior. This Seeker visited several churches on his journey to Christ, many of them like this one. Most of the teaching he received in those places could be condensed to one statement, "God is really mad, you are really bad, so find a way to do better." Hope level: ZERO.

Jesus didn't mince words about those who design and promote religious systems. He said, *"They crush people with unbearable religious demands and never lift a finger to ease the burden. Everything they do is for show"* (Matthew 23:4-5). One man said, "I came to church broken, needing God, and it's like the church laid a pallet of bricks on my back." Once a religious system is in place, people use it to judge others and feel more righteous (self-righteousness). Christ said, *"What sorrow awaits you teachers of religious law…for you cross land and sea to make one convert, and then you turn that person into twice the child of hell you yourselves are!"* (Matthew 23:15). Jesus was no fan of religious systems. A simple reading of the twenty-third chapter of Matthew makes that obvious. He certainly did NOT come to give us a new religious system, He came to be our source of forgiveness and a beautiful relationship with a gracious God.

The Impact Journey: Trail Marker One

The Seeker decides he does NOT want a religious system. He wants a Savior. He wants a relationship with God. This changes him somehow, at the core.

Key Bible Verse:

"Christ suffered for our sins once for all time. He never sinned, but he died for sinners to bring you safely home to God. He suffered physical death, but he was raised to life in the Spirit."   1 Peter 3:18

Jesus said, "It is finished!" in John 19:30. What did He mean?

Jesus lived as our example and died as the sacrifice for all our sins and shame. After paying that awful price, he proclaimed this amazing word, *tetelestai* (tuh-tel-es-tie). This word is generally translated, "It is finished," but was also used as an accounting term and translated, "paid in full!" C.H. Spurgeon wrote about this beautiful, one-word declaration, saying it is, "an ocean of meaning in a drop of language...IT IS FINISHED is the most charming note in all of Calvary's music. The fire has passed upon the Lamb. He has borne the whole of the wrath that was due to His people. This is the royal dish of the feast of love." You see, after living as our example, Jesus bore the full burden and paid the full price for our sins. It is finished. Nothing more is needed. Forgiveness and relationship with God is a pure gift that we receive by faith. John 1:12 says, *"But to all who believed him and accepted him, he gave the right to become children of God."* Christ's accomplishment is not something to be earned, it is a GIFT to be received.

Your Impact Log

Today's Chapter: **Date:**

Truth and Promises:
Father, what are the truths and promises you have for me today?

_____

_____

_____

_____

_____

Adjustments and Assignments:
Holy Spirit, what adjustments and assignments do you have for me today?

_____

_____

_____

Support and Encouragement
What support or encouragement do I need to share or experience today?

_____

_____

_____

Prayer
You can turn these experiences into a prayer here or record prayer needs you are lifting to God.

_____

_____

_____

_____

Your Impact Log

Today's Chapter: **Date:**

Truth and Promises:
Father, what are the truths and promises you have for me today?

_____

_____

_____

_____

Adjustments and Assignments:
Holy Spirit, what adjustments and assignments do you have for me today?

_____

_____

_____

Support and Encouragement
What support or encouragement do I need to share or experience today?

_____

_____

_____

Prayer
You can turn these experiences into a prayer here or record prayer needs you are lifting to God.

_____

_____

_____

_____

Your Impact Log

Today's Chapter: **Date:**

Truth and Promises:
Father, what are the truths and promises you have for me today?

_____

_____

_____

_____

Adjustments and Assignments:
Holy Spirit, what adjustments and assignments do you have for me today?

_____

_____

_____

Support and Encouragement
What support or encouragement do I need to share or experience today?

_____

_____

_____

Prayer
You can turn these experiences into a prayer here or record prayer needs you are lifting to God.

_____

_____

_____

_____

Your Impact Log

Today's Chapter: **Date:**

Truth and Promises:
Father, what are the truths and promises you have for me today?

_____

_____

_____

_____

_____

Adjustments and Assignments:
Holy Spirit, what adjustments and assignments do you have for me today?

_____

_____

_____

Support and Encouragement
What support or encouragement do I need to share or experience today?

_____

_____

_____

Prayer
You can turn these experiences into a prayer here or record prayer needs you are lifting to God.

_____

_____

_____

_____

Your Impact Log

Today's Chapter: **Date:**

Truth and Promises:

Father, what are the truths and promises you have for me today?

_____

_____

_____

_____

_____

Adjustments and Assignments:

Holy Spirit, what adjustments and assignments do you have for me today?

_____

_____

_____

Support and Encouragement

What support or encouragement do I need to share or experience today?

_____

_____

_____

Prayer

You can turn these experiences into a prayer here or record prayer needs you are lifting to God.

_____

_____

_____

_____

The Impact Journey: Trail Marker Two

The Seeker realizes the importance of receiving Christ. He calls out to the Lord in prayer to express faith in all that Christ accomplished for him. His prayer goes something like this:

Lord Jesus, I need you in my life. I'm so grateful that you lived as my example. I believe that you died for all my sins. You rose from death to prove you are my source of forgiveness. I receive all that you did for me as a gift. You gave your perfect life for me. Now I am giving my life to you. You are my Savior and Lord. Help me live in a way that others can see you through my life. Amen.

Key Bible Verse:
"God saved you by his grace when you believed. And you can't take credit for this; it is a gift from God. 9 Salvation is not a reward for the good things we have done, so none of us can boast about it. 10 For we are God's masterpiece. He has created us anew in Christ Jesus, so we can do the good things he planned for us long ago."

Ephesians 2:8-10

Salvation means we have complete forgiveness and heaven is our eternal destination. It is not "a reward for the good things we have done." It comes by trusting in the achievement of Jesus Christ. Verse 10 in this passage is not about eternal salvation, it is about living out *our purpose* in the here and now! We were made by God ("we are God's masterpiece") to do good things, things planned out long ago.

Your Impact Log

Today's Chapter: **Date:**

Truth and Promises:
Father, what are the truths and promises you have for me today?

_____

_____

_____

_____

_____

Adjustments and Assignments:
Holy Spirit, what adjustments and assignments do you have for me today?

_____

_____

_____

Support and Encouragement
What support or encouragement do I need to share or experience today?

_____

_____

_____

Prayer
You can turn these experiences into a prayer here or record prayer needs you are lifting to God.

_____

_____

_____

_____

Your Impact Log

Today's Chapter: **Date:**

Truth and Promises:
Father, what are the truths and promises you have for me today?

_____

_____

_____

_____

_____

Adjustments and Assignments:
Holy Spirit, what adjustments and assignments do you have for me today?

_____

_____

_____

_____

Support and Encouragement
What support or encouragement do I need to share or experience today?

_____

_____

_____

_____

Prayer
You can turn these experiences into a prayer here or record prayer needs you are lifting to God.

_____

_____

_____

_____

Your Impact Log

Today's Chapter: **Date:**

Truth and Promises:
Father, what are the truths and promises you have for me today?

_____

_____

_____

_____

_____

Adjustments and Assignments:
Holy Spirit, what adjustments and assignments do you have for me today?

_____

_____

_____

Support and Encouragement
What support or encouragement do I need to share or experience today?

_____

_____

_____

Prayer
You can turn these experiences into a prayer here or record prayer needs you are lifting to God.

_____

_____

_____

Your Impact Log

Today's Chapter: **Date:**

Truth and Promises:
Father, what are the truths and promises you have for me today?

_____

_____

_____

_____

_____

Adjustments and Assignments:
Holy Spirit, what adjustments and assignments do you have for me today?

_____

_____

_____

_____

Support and Encouragement
What support or encouragement do I need to share or experience today?

_____

_____

_____

_____

Prayer
You can turn these experiences into a prayer here or record prayer needs you are lifting to God.

_____

_____

_____

_____

Your Impact Log

Today's Chapter: **Date:**

Truth and Promises:
Father, what are the truths and promises you have for me today?

_____

_____

_____

_____

_____

Adjustments and Assignments:
Holy Spirit, what adjustments and assignments do you have for me today?

_____

_____

_____

Support and Encouragement
What support or encouragement do I need to share or experience today?

_____

_____

_____

Prayer
You can turn these experiences into a prayer here or record prayer needs you are lifting to God.

_____

_____

_____

_____

The Impact Journey: Trail Marker Three (a)

The Seeker becomes a Disciple (life-long follower of Christ) who becomes aware that God has things for Him to do.

*---**Breakdown---:** The Disciple starts doing things for God. Everything he can think of. He starts attending every church service, helping everyone with a need. Soon, he is tired, burned out, broken down, and confused.*

It's natural for someone, having experienced the grace of God, to want to do things for Him. However, we must think about *who He is*. He is God. Almighty God. All-knowing God. He spoke the universe into existence and holds everything together by the word of His power (Colossians 1:17). He doesn't need us to come up with things to do for Him. He is always at work. He always blesses His own work. He allows us to have assignments within His work, if we listen. We just need to learn how to receive those assignments. They come in the context of relationship, connecting with God.

Key Bible Verse:

Then Jesus said, "Come to me, all of you who are weary and carry heavy burdens, and I will give you rest. Take my yoke upon you. Let me teach you, because I am humble and gentle at heart, and you will find rest for your souls. For my yoke is easy to bear, and the burden I give you is light."

Matthew 11:28-30

Your Impact Log

Today's Chapter: **Date:**

Truth and Promises:
Father, what are the truths and promises you have for me today?

_____

_____

_____

_____

_____

Adjustments and Assignments:
Holy Spirit, what adjustments and assignments do you have for me today?

_____

_____

_____

_____

Support and Encouragement
What support or encouragement do I need to share or experience today?

_____

_____

_____

_____

Prayer
You can turn these experiences into a prayer here or record prayer needs you are lifting to God.

_____

_____

_____

_____

Your Impact Log

Today's Chapter: **Date:**

Truth and Promises:
Father, what are the truths and promises you have for me today?

_____

_____

_____

_____

_____

Adjustments and Assignments:
Holy Spirit, what adjustments and assignments do you have for me today?

_____

_____

_____

Support and Encouragement
What support or encouragement do I need to share or experience today?

_____

_____

_____

Prayer
You can turn these experiences into a prayer here or record prayer needs you are lifting to God.

_____

_____

_____

Your Impact Log

Today's Chapter: **Date:**

Truth and Promises:

Father, what are the truths and promises you have for me today?

_____

_____

_____

_____

_____

Adjustments and Assignments:

Holy Spirit, what adjustments and assignments do you have for me today?

_____

_____

_____

Support and Encouragement

What support or encouragement do I need to share or experience today?

_____

_____

_____

Prayer

You can turn these experiences into a prayer here or record prayer needs you are lifting to God.

_____

_____

_____

Your Impact Log

Today's Chapter: **Date:**

Truth and Promises:
Father, what are the truths and promises you have for me today?

_____

_____

_____

_____

_____

Adjustments and Assignments:
Holy Spirit, what adjustments and assignments do you have for me today?

_____

_____

_____

_____

Support and Encouragement
What support or encouragement do I need to share or experience today?

_____

_____

_____

_____

Prayer
You can turn these experiences into a prayer here or record prayer needs you are lifting to God.

_____

_____

_____

_____

Your Impact Log

Today's Chapter: **Date:**

Truth and Promises:
Father, what are the truths and promises you have for me today?

_____

_____

_____

_____

_____

Adjustments and Assignments:
Holy Spirit, what adjustments and assignments do you have for me today?

_____

_____

_____

Support and Encouragement
What support or encouragement do I need to share or experience today?

_____

_____

_____

Prayer
You can turn these experiences into a prayer here or record prayer needs you are lifting to God.

_____

_____

_____

_____

The Impact Journey: Trail Marker Three (b)

The Disciple realizes that what God wants most is not accomplishment, *but relationship*. He realizes that a relationship is about closeness and communication. He discovers the promise that God is always near. And just acknowledging His presence can bring power and direction (Proverbs 3:5-6).

God is always close, but people don't always acknowledge His presence. The apostle Paul, when introducing philosophers in Athens, Greece to Christ, said this about God, *"His purpose was for the nations to seek after God and perhaps feel their way toward him and find him—though he is not far from any one of us. For in him we live and move and exist. As some of your own poets have said, 'We are his offspring,'"* (Acts 17:27-28). God is never far from us. So, how do we connect with Him each day and receive what He has for us? God wants to meet with us and give us special blessings each day! These blessings are everything we need to endure, overcome, and experience victories in life. These blessings come in the form of truth and promises.

Truth

Jesus said, "...*you will know the truth, and the truth will set you free.*" John 8:32

Remember, a truth is an instruction designed to guide thought and behavior. In other words, principles to avoid pitfalls. We receive Christ into our lives for the salvation of our souls. But we receive the truth of His teaching each day to save us from the traps and pitfalls of godless living. We're held back, and sometimes held captive, by believing lies about who we are and who God is. We need to be set free from these falsehoods.

Your Impact Log

Today's Chapter: **Date:**

Truth and Promises:
Father, what are the truths and promises you have for me today?

_____

_____

_____

_____

_____

Adjustments and Assignments:
Holy Spirit, what adjustments and assignments do you have for me today?

_____

_____

_____

_____

Support and Encouragement
What support or encouragement do I need to share or experience today?

_____

_____

_____

_____

Prayer
You can turn these experiences into a prayer here or record prayer needs you are lifting to God.

_____

_____

_____

_____

Your Impact Log

Today's Chapter: **Date:**

Truth and Promises:
Father, what are the truths and promises you have for me today?

_____

_____

_____

_____

_____

Adjustments and Assignments:
Holy Spirit, what adjustments and assignments do you have for me today?

_____

_____

_____

_____

Support and Encouragement
What support or encouragement do I need to share or experience today?

_____

_____

_____

_____

Prayer
You can turn these experiences into a prayer here or record prayer needs you are lifting to God.

_____

_____

_____

_____

Your Impact Log

Today's Chapter: **Date:**

Truth and Promises:

Father, what are the truths and promises you have for me today?

_____

_____

_____

_____

Adjustments and Assignments:

Holy Spirit, what adjustments and assignments do you have for me today?

_____

_____

_____

Support and Encouragement

What support or encouragement do I need to share or experience today?

_____

_____

_____

Prayer

You can turn these experiences into a prayer here or record prayer needs you are lifting to God.

_____

_____

_____

_____

Your Impact Log

Today's Chapter: **Date:**

Truth and Promises:

Father, what are the truths and promises you have for me today?

_____

_____

_____

_____

_____

Adjustments and Assignments:

Holy Spirit, what adjustments and assignments do you have for me today?

_____

_____

_____

Support and Encouragement

What support or encouragement do I need to share or experience today?

_____

_____

_____

Prayer

You can turn these experiences into a prayer here or record prayer needs you are lifting to God.

_____

_____

_____

Your Impact Log

Today's Chapter: **Date:**

Truth and Promises:

Father, what are the truths and promises you have for me today?

_____

_____

_____

_____

Adjustments and Assignments:

Holy Spirit, what adjustments and assignments do you have for me today?

_____

_____

_____

Support and Encouragement

What support or encouragement do I need to share or experience today?

_____

_____

_____

Prayer

You can turn these experiences into a prayer here or record prayer needs you are lifting to God.

_____

_____

_____

The Impact Journey: Trail Marker Four

The Disciple's sense of self changes. He is receiving a new identity in Christ. He's no longer simply what he has done, or what has been done to him. He begins to believe what the Bible says about him. He lets the Bible shape what he believes about himself, not the voices of accusation in his head. He lets the words of Christ shape what he believes about God. He's beginning to live out the new identity given to him by Christ with a growing understanding of the goodness of God.

Key Bible Verse:

"So, we have stopped evaluating others from a human point of view. At one time we thought of Christ merely from a human point of view. How differently we know him now! This means that anyone who belongs to Christ has become a new person. The old life is gone; a new life has begun!'

2 Corinthians 5:17

Our new identity in Christ is further developed each time we see a truth or promise that shapes our 'I am' statements. For example, consider Ephesians 1:3-5
3 All praise to God, the Father of our Lord Jesus Christ, who has blessed us with every spiritual blessing in the heavenly realms because we are united with Christ. 4 Even before he made the world, God loved us and chose us in Christ to be holy and without fault in his eyes. 5 God decided in advance to adopt us into his own family by bringing us to himself through Jesus Christ. This is what he wanted to do, and it gave him great pleasure.

From these brief verses I can say:
I AM '...blessed with every spiritual blessing in the heavenly realms'
I AM '...united with Christ.'
I AM '...loved by God'

I AM '...chosen by God'
I AM '...holy and without fault in His eyes'
I AM '...adopted by God'
I AM '...in the family of God'

These, and hundreds of other statements in the New Testament, become our new identity in Christ as we learn them, and embrace them by faith. They empower us to live for Him in this world. It is who we are!

Your Impact Log

Today's Chapter: **Date:**

Truth and Promises:

Father, what are the truths and promises you have for me today?

_____

_____

_____

_____

Adjustments and Assignments:

Holy Spirit, what adjustments and assignments do you have for me today?

_____

_____

_____

Support and Encouragement

What support or encouragement do I need to share or experience today?

_____

_____

_____

Prayer

You can turn these experiences into a prayer here or record prayer needs you are lifting to God.

_____

_____

_____

Your Impact Log

Today's Chapter: **Date:**

Truth and Promises:
Father, what are the truths and promises you have for me today?

_____

_____

_____

_____

_____

Adjustments and Assignments:
Holy Spirit, what adjustments and assignments do you have for me today?

_____

_____

_____

Support and Encouragement
What support or encouragement do I need to share or experience today?

_____

_____

_____

Prayer
You can turn these experiences into a prayer here or record prayer needs you are lifting to God.

_____

_____

_____

_____

Your Impact Log

Today's Chapter: **Date:**

Truth and Promises:
Father, what are the truths and promises you have for me today?

_____

_____

_____

_____

_____

Adjustments and Assignments:
Holy Spirit, what adjustments and assignments do you have for me today?

_____

_____

_____

_____

Support and Encouragement
What support or encouragement do I need to share or experience today?

_____

_____

_____

_____

Prayer
You can turn these experiences into a prayer here or record prayer needs you are lifting to God.

_____

_____

_____

_____

Your Impact Log

Today's Chapter: **Date:**

Truth and Promises:

Father, what are the truths and promises you have for me today?

_____

_____

_____

_____

_____

Adjustments and Assignments:

Holy Spirit, what adjustments and assignments do you have for me today?

_____

_____

_____

Support and Encouragement

What support or encouragement do I need to share or experience today?

_____

_____

_____

Prayer

You can turn these experiences into a prayer here or record prayer needs you are lifting to God.

_____

_____

_____

_____

Your Impact Log

Today's Chapter: **Date:**

Truth and Promises:
Father, what are the truths and promises you have for me today?

_____

_____

_____

_____

Adjustments and Assignments:
Holy Spirit, what adjustments and assignments do you have for me today?

_____

_____

_____

Support and Encouragement
What support or encouragement do I need to share or experience today?

_____

_____

_____

Prayer
You can turn these experiences into a prayer here or record prayer needs you are lifting to God.

_____

_____

_____

The Impact Journey: Trail Marker Five

The Disciple realizes that the best lived life is empowered by God's promises. These 'great and precious promises' are always connected to challenges we face. They are the access point to God's provision for all things. Anything we need to escape from, overcome, or persevere through is made possible through faith in the promises of God.

Promises

"And because of his glory and excellence, he has given us great and precious promises. These are the promises that enable you to share his divine nature and escape the world's corruption caused by human desires."

2 Peter 1:4

There are 7,487 verses in the Bible that contain promises from God to believers. Those promises are the treasure that belongs to all who receive Christ (2 Corinthians 1:20). The promises are the blessings of God's grace, empowering us to be overcomers in Christ.

Your Impact Log

Today's Chapter: **Date:**

Truth and Promises:
Father, what are the truths and promises you have for me today?

_____

_____

_____

_____

Adjustments and Assignments:
Holy Spirit, what adjustments and assignments do you have for me today?

_____

_____

_____

Support and Encouragement
What support or encouragement do I need to share or experience today?

_____

_____

_____

Prayer
You can turn these experiences into a prayer here or record prayer needs you are lifting to God.

_____

_____

_____

_____

Your Impact Log

Today's Chapter: **Date:**

Truth and Promises:

Father, what are the truths and promises you have for me today?

_____

_____

_____

_____

_____

Adjustments and Assignments:

Holy Spirit, what adjustments and assignments do you have for me today?

_____

_____

_____

Support and Encouragement

What support or encouragement do I need to share or experience today?

_____

_____

_____

Prayer

You can turn these experiences into a prayer here or record prayer needs you are lifting to God.

_____

_____

_____

Your Impact Log

Today's Chapter: **Date:**

Truth and Promises:
Father, what are the truths and promises you have for me today?

_____

_____

_____

_____

_____

Adjustments and Assignments:
Holy Spirit, what adjustments and assignments do you have for me today?

_____

_____

_____

Support and Encouragement
What support or encouragement do I need to share or experience today?

_____

_____

_____

Prayer
You can turn these experiences into a prayer here or record prayer needs you are lifting to God.

_____

_____

_____

Your Impact Log

Today's Chapter: **Date:**

Truth and Promises:
Father, what are the truths and promises you have for me today?

_____

_____

_____

_____

Adjustments and Assignments:
Holy Spirit, what adjustments and assignments do you have for me today?

_____

_____

_____

Support and Encouragement
What support or encouragement do I need to share or experience today?

_____

_____

_____

Prayer
You can turn these experiences into a prayer here or record prayer needs you are lifting to God.

_____

_____

_____

_____

Your Impact Log

Today's Chapter: **Date:**

Truth and Promises:
Father, what are the truths and promises you have for me today?

_____

_____

_____

_____

Adjustments and Assignments:
Holy Spirit, what adjustments and assignments do you have for me today?

_____

_____

_____

Support and Encouragement
What support or encouragement do I need to share or experience today?

_____

_____

_____

Prayer
You can turn these experiences into a prayer here or record prayer needs you are lifting to God.

_____

_____

_____

_____

Impact Journey: Trail Marker Six

The Disciple understands the Holy Spirit is within him, ready to make adjustments and assignments, but he must yield to His leadership and ask for it.

Daily Adjustments and Assignments

The Bible says that God the Father is on His throne of grace in heaven (Hebrews 4:16). Jesus Christ is seated at his right hand (Hebrews 10:12). Yet God is in us. 'God in us' is called the Holy Spirit. Jesus described him as our Advocate, Comforter, Guide, and Teacher. He is in every believer. And He has a specific purpose for His work in our lives. It is to magnify Jesus in us and through us to others (John 16:14).

Key Verses:

"But I tell you the truth, it is for your benefit that I am going away. Unless I go away, the Advocate will not come to you; but if I go, I will send Him to you."

John 16:7

"However, when the Spirit of truth comes, He will guide you into all truth."

John 16:13

Adjustments

God wants Christ to shine through our lives. This can only happen when we are yielded to the Holy Spirit's leadership and He produces the 'fruit' of Christlikeness in us. There is a force working against that goal, and it stays with us until we see Christ, face to face. The Bible describes it as 'the flesh' or 'carnal nature'. It's the ancient Greek word (the language of the New Testament) 'sarkos'. Galatians chapter five describes the tension between the work of the Holy Spirit in us, and

this ancient, tidal force, drawing us away from this good and beautiful work.
"So I say, let the Holy Spirit guide your lives. Then you won't be doing what your sinful nature (sarkos) craves."
Galatians 5:16

There are appetites given by God that are part of our human experience. They are gifts to be enjoyed. But when these appetites become cravings that drive our actions, they can make use others and destroy life's most precious relationships. We were created to love people and use things. Cravings and selfish ambitions cause us to do the opposite: loving things and using people. We have a daily battle to fight against this. The Bible calls it the "the good fight" (2 Timothy 4:7). We yield ourselves to the Holy Spirit's leadership by asking Him to lead. We ask Him to reveal the adjustments He wants to make in us, so Christ can shine more brightly through us.

Assignments

The Holy Spirit will give us daily assignments if we ask for them. Assignments from the Holy Spirit are always actions that impact people. Often we say, "the assignments of the Holy Spirit usually have names." Sometimes the Holy Spirit makes an assignment clear while you are having your devotion time. Other times, assignments come during the day and you are sensitive to them because you've spent time with God. The important thing to remember is that the Holy Spirit works by invitation. "So I say, let the Holy Spirit guide your lives..." (Galatians 5:16a). We must invite the Holy Spirit to make His adjustments and give His assignments. If this is what we genuinely want, we'll experience His magnificent work. He is God and He always blesses His own work (Ephesians 3:20)!

Support and Encouragement

Living for God is a team sport. Jesus never sent any disciple to do anything alone (Mark 10:1). We have four books about the life and teachings of Jesus in the Bible: Matthew, Mark, Luke, and John. Why? Because one person's perspective is not enough. We need to get and give encouragement to live for Christ in the world.

"Let us think of ways to motivate one another to acts of love and good works. And let us not neglect our meeting together, as some people do, but encourage one another, especially now that the day of his return is drawing near."   Hebrews 10:24-25

\

Your Impact Log

Today's Chapter: **Date:**

Truth and Promises:
Father, what are the truths and promises you have for me today?

_____

_____

_____

_____

Adjustments and Assignments:
Holy Spirit, what adjustments and assignments do you have for me today?

_____

_____

_____

Support and Encouragement
What support or encouragement do I need to share or experience today?

_____

_____

_____

Prayer
You can turn these experiences into a prayer here or record prayer needs you are lifting to God.

_____

_____

_____

Your Impact Log

Today's Chapter: **Date:**

Truth and Promises:
Father, what are the truths and promises you have for me today?

_____

_____

_____

_____

_____

Adjustments and Assignments:
Holy Spirit, what adjustments and assignments do you have for me today?

_____

_____

_____

Support and Encouragement
What support or encouragement do I need to share or experience today?

_____

_____

_____

Prayer
You can turn these experiences into a prayer here or record prayer needs you are lifting to God.

_____

_____

_____

_____

Your Impact Log

Today's Chapter: **Date:**

Truth and Promises:
Father, what are the truths and promises you have for me today?

_____

_____

_____

_____

_____

Adjustments and Assignments:
Holy Spirit, what adjustments and assignments do you have for me today?

_____

_____

_____

_____

Support and Encouragement
What support or encouragement do I need to share or experience today?

_____

_____

_____

_____

Prayer
You can turn these experiences into a prayer here or record prayer needs you are lifting to God.

_____

_____

_____

_____

Your Impact Log

Today's Chapter: **Date:**

Truth and Promises:
Father, what are the truths and promises you have for me today?

_____

_____

_____

_____

_____

Adjustments and Assignments:
Holy Spirit, what adjustments and assignments do you have for me today?

_____

_____

_____

Support and Encouragement
What support or encouragement do I need to share or experience today?

_____

_____

_____

Prayer
You can turn these experiences into a prayer here or record prayer needs you are lifting to God.

_____

_____

_____

Your Impact Log

Today's Chapter: **Date:**

Truth and Promises:
Father, what are the truths and promises you have for me today?

_____

_____

_____

_____

_____

Adjustments and Assignments:
Holy Spirit, what adjustments and assignments do you have for me today?

_____

_____

_____

_____

Support and Encouragement
What support or encouragement do I need to share or experience today?

_____

_____

_____

_____

Prayer
You can turn these experiences into a prayer here or record prayer needs you are lifting to God.

_____

_____

_____

_____

The Impact Journey: Trail Marker Seven

The Disciple begins to experience deep friendship with God.

Aristotle, the great, Greek philosopher, said friendship requires people to have things in common. It begins with the words , "You too?" He concluded that no human can be a friend of God because we don't have anything in common with him. He was right on the first observation and wrong on the conclusion.

How can we be friends of Almighty God?

'And so it happened just as the Scriptures say: "Abraham believed God, and God counted him as righteous because of his faith." He was even called the friend of God.'   James 2:23

First: The Nature of God

The God of the Bible is tri-personal. He has always existed as a unified relationship: Father, Son, and Holy Spirit. We call this the Trinity. It means that God is a friendship. He is not uni-personal. If God was uni-personal and created everything, he would have been power before he was love. Power would be primary, and love would be secondary. But that's never the case with God! Love is the primary character trait of God and influences all other aspects of His character (1 John 4:8). God is triune. He is a friendship. That is primary. God is love. God didn't become this; it has always been His nature. In the first chapter of the Bible, when God was creating human beings, He said, "Let us make man in our image," (Genesis 1:26). We are the imago dei, the image of God. This means we have the capacity for deep relationship and the ability to reflect God's character traits (Galatians 5:22-23).

Next: Redemption, the Cosmic Act of Friendship!

"He was made like us in every way..." Hebrews
John 15 "The greatest act of friendship possible is to lay down your life for your friends." No other God became vulnerable, mortal, and like us, to take us by the hand as our example, then suffer horribly in our place for our forgiveness and redemption.

Jesus became like us in EVERY way. In my temptations? Yes. In my rejection... Yes! Even in my lostness?...Yes! He felt our lostness when all sin of all time was placed on Him (2 Corinthians 5:21). He expressed this when He cried, "My God, my God, why have you forsaken me?" (Matthew 27:46). He never sinned, but felt the full weight of ours.

Relational Agreement

Let's say you have a big brother who's a genius. He loves you more than life itself and only wants the very best for your life. If that brother says to you one day, "I want to tell you the three things that are most important for you to do to have a good life." Would it make sense for you to pay attention and make an effort to do those things? We have the best big brother ever in Jesus Christ! (Hebrews 2:11; Romans 8:29; Mark 3:34).

One stunning aspect of Jesus Christ, and our friendship with God, is that Christ makes himself our elder brother. He is the ultimate genius. He literally loves us to death. He tells us in the NT what is important to believe and do as we follow him. Biblical obedience is just agreeing with our Elder Brother about what is important in life.

'So now Jesus and the ones he makes holy have the same Father. That is why Jesus is not ashamed to call them his brothers and sisters. '

Hebrews 2:11

For God knew his people in advance, and he chose them to become like his Son, so that his Son would be the firstborn among many brothers and sisters.   Romans 8:29

Then he looked at those around him and said, "Look, these are my mother and brothers. 35 Anyone who does God's will is my brother and sister and mother."   Mark 3:34

Your Impact Log

Today's Chapter: **Date:**

Truth and Promises:
Father, what are the truths and promises you have for me today?

_____

_____

_____

_____

Adjustments and Assignments:
Holy Spirit, what adjustments and assignments do you have for me today?

_____

_____

_____

Support and Encouragement
What support or encouragement do I need to share or experience today?

_____

_____

_____

Prayer
You can turn these experiences into a prayer here or record prayer needs you are lifting to God.

_____

_____

_____

Your Impact Log

Today's Chapter: **Date:**

Truth and Promises:
Father, what are the truths and promises you have for me today?

_____

_____

_____

_____

_____

Adjustments and Assignments:
Holy Spirit, what adjustments and assignments do you have for me today?

_____

_____

_____

Support and Encouragement
What support or encouragement do I need to share or experience today?

_____

_____

_____

Prayer
You can turn these experiences into a prayer here or record prayer needs you are lifting to God.

_____

_____

_____

Your Impact Log

Today's Chapter: **Date:**

Truth and Promises:
Father, what are the truths and promises you have for me today?

_____

_____

_____

_____

Adjustments and Assignments:
Holy Spirit, what adjustments and assignments do you have for me today?

_____

_____

_____

Support and Encouragement
What support or encouragement do I need to share or experience today?

_____

_____

_____

Prayer
You can turn these experiences into a prayer here or record prayer needs you are lifting to God.

_____

_____

_____

Your Impact Log

Today's Chapter: **Date:**

Truth and Promises:

Father, what are the truths and promises you have for me today?

_____

_____

_____

_____

Adjustments and Assignments:

Holy Spirit, what adjustments and assignments do you have for me today?

_____

_____

_____

Support and Encouragement

What support or encouragement do I need to share or experience today?

_____

_____

_____

Prayer

You can turn these experiences into a prayer here or record prayer needs you are lifting to God.

_____

_____

_____

_____

Your Impact Log

Today's Chapter: **Date:**

Truth and Promises:
Father, what are the truths and promises you have for me today?

_____

_____

_____

_____

Adjustments and Assignments:
Holy Spirit, what adjustments and assignments do you have for me today?

_____

_____

_____

Support and Encouragement
What support or encouragement do I need to share or experience today?

_____

_____

_____

Prayer
You can turn these experiences into a prayer here or record prayer needs you are lifting to God.

_____

_____

_____

Your Impact Log

Today's Chapter: **Date:**

Truth and Promises:

Father, what are the truths and promises you have for me today?

_____

_____

_____

_____

Adjustments and Assignments:

Holy Spirit, what adjustments and assignments do you have for me today?

_____

_____

_____

Support and Encouragement

What support or encouragement do I need to share or experience today?

_____

_____

_____

Prayer

You can turn these experiences into a prayer here or record prayer needs you are lifting to God.

_____

_____

_____

Your Impact Log

Today's Chapter: **Date:**

Truth and Promises:
Father, what are the truths and promises you have for me today?

_____

_____

_____

_____

_____

Adjustments and Assignments:
Holy Spirit, what adjustments and assignments do you have for me today?

_____

_____

_____

_____

Support and Encouragement
What support or encouragement do I need to share or experience today?

_____

_____

_____

_____

Prayer
You can turn these experiences into a prayer here or record prayer needs you are lifting to God.

_____

_____

_____

_____

Your Impact Log

Today's Chapter: **Date:**

Truth and Promises:

Father, what are the truths and promises you have for me today?

_____

_____

_____

_____

_____

Adjustments and Assignments:

Holy Spirit, what adjustments and assignments do you have for me today?

_____

_____

_____

_____

Support and Encouragement

What support or encouragement do I need to share or experience today?

_____

_____

_____

_____

Prayer

You can turn these experiences into a prayer here or record prayer needs you are lifting to God.

_____

_____

_____

_____

Your Impact Log

Today's Chapter: **Date:**

Truth and Promises:
Father, what are the truths and promises you have for me today?

_____

_____

_____

_____

_____

Adjustments and Assignments:
Holy Spirit, what adjustments and assignments do you have for me today?

_____

_____

_____

_____

Support and Encouragement
What support or encouragement do I need to share or experience today?

_____

_____

_____

_____

Prayer
You can turn these experiences into a prayer here or record prayer needs you are lifting to God.

_____

_____

_____

_____

Your Impact Log

Today's Chapter: **Date:**

Truth and Promises:

Father, what are the truths and promises you have for me today?

_____

_____

_____

_____

_____

Adjustments and Assignments:

Holy Spirit, what adjustments and assignments do you have for me today?

_____

_____

_____

Support and Encouragement

What support or encouragement do I need to share or experience today?

_____

_____

_____

Prayer

You can turn these experiences into a prayer here or record prayer needs you are lifting to God.

_____

_____

_____

_____

Your Impact Log

Today's Chapter: **Date:**

Truth and Promises:

Father, what are the truths and promises you have for me today?

_____

_____

_____

_____

Adjustments and Assignments:

Holy Spirit, what adjustments and assignments do you have for me today?

_____

_____

_____

Support and Encouragement

What support or encouragement do I need to share or experience today?

_____

_____

_____

Prayer

You can turn these experiences into a prayer here or record prayer needs you are lifting to God.

_____

_____

_____

_____

Your Impact Log

Today's Chapter: **Date:**

Truth and Promises:
Father, what are the truths and promises you have for me today?

_____

_____

_____

_____

_____

Adjustments and Assignments:
Holy Spirit, what adjustments and assignments do you have for me today?

_____

_____

_____

Support and Encouragement
What support or encouragement do I need to share or experience today?

_____

_____

_____

Prayer
You can turn these experiences into a prayer here or record prayer needs you are lifting to God.

_____

_____

_____

_____

Your Impact Log

Today's Chapter: **Date:**

Truth and Promises:

Father, what are the truths and promises you have for me today?

_____

_____

_____

_____

_____

Adjustments and Assignments:

Holy Spirit, what adjustments and assignments do you have for me today?

_____

_____

_____

Support and Encouragement

What support or encouragement do I need to share or experience today?

_____

_____

_____

Prayer

You can turn these experiences into a prayer here or record prayer needs you are lifting to God.

_____

_____

_____

_____

Your Impact Log

Today's Chapter: **Date:**

Truth and Promises:
Father, what are the truths and promises you have for me today?

_____

_____

_____

_____

Adjustments and Assignments:
Holy Spirit, what adjustments and assignments do you have for me today?

_____

_____

_____

Support and Encouragement
What support or encouragement do I need to share or experience today?

_____

_____

_____

Prayer
You can turn these experiences into a prayer here or record prayer needs you are lifting to God.

_____

_____

_____

_____

Your Impact Log

Today's Chapter: **Date:**

Truth and Promises:
Father, what are the truths and promises you have for me today?

_____

_____

_____

_____

_____

Adjustments and Assignments:
Holy Spirit, what adjustments and assignments do you have for me today?

_____

_____

_____

_____

Support and Encouragement
What support or encouragement do I need to share or experience today?

_____

_____

_____

_____

Prayer
You can turn these experiences into a prayer here or record prayer needs you are lifting to God.

_____

_____

_____

_____

Your Impact Log

Today's Chapter: **Date:**

Truth and Promises:
Father, what are the truths and promises you have for me today?

_____

_____

_____

_____

_____

Adjustments and Assignments:
Holy Spirit, what adjustments and assignments do you have for me today?

_____

_____

_____

_____

Support and Encouragement
What support or encouragement do I need to share or experience today?

_____

_____

_____

_____

Prayer
You can turn these experiences into a prayer here or record prayer needs you are lifting to God.

_____

_____

_____

_____

Your Impact Log

Today's Chapter: **Date:**

Truth and Promises:
Father, what are the truths and promises you have for me today?

_____

_____

_____

_____

_____

Adjustments and Assignments:
Holy Spirit, what adjustments and assignments do you have for me today?

_____

_____

_____

Support and Encouragement
What support or encouragement do I need to share or experience today?

_____

_____

_____

Prayer
You can turn these experiences into a prayer here or record prayer needs you are lifting to God.

_____

_____

_____

Your Impact Log

Today's Chapter: **Date:**

Truth and Promises:
Father, what are the truths and promises you have for me today?

_____

_____

_____

_____

_____

Adjustments and Assignments:
Holy Spirit, what adjustments and assignments do you have for me today?

_____

_____

_____

Support and Encouragement
What support or encouragement do I need to share or experience today?

_____

_____

_____

Prayer
You can turn these experiences into a prayer here or record prayer needs you are lifting to God.

_____

_____

_____

_____

Your Impact Log

Today's Chapter: **Date:**

Truth and Promises:
Father, what are the truths and promises you have for me today?

_____

_____

_____

_____

Adjustments and Assignments:
Holy Spirit, what adjustments and assignments do you have for me today?

_____

_____

_____

Support and Encouragement
What support or encouragement do I need to share or experience today?

_____

_____

_____

Prayer
You can turn these experiences into a prayer here or record prayer needs you are lifting to God.

_____

_____

_____

Your Impact Log

Today's Chapter: **Date:**

Truth and Promises:
Father, what are the truths and promises you have for me today?

_____

_____

_____

_____

_____

Adjustments and Assignments:
Holy Spirit, what adjustments and assignments do you have for me today?

_____

_____

_____

Support and Encouragement
What support or encouragement do I need to share or experience today?

_____

_____

_____

Prayer
You can turn these experiences into a prayer here or record prayer needs you are lifting to God.

_____

_____

_____

Your Impact Log

Today's Chapter: **Date:**

Truth and Promises:
Father, what are the truths and promises you have for me today?

_____

_____

_____

_____

_____

Adjustments and Assignments:
Holy Spirit, what adjustments and assignments do you have for me today?

_____

_____

_____

_____

Support and Encouragement
What support or encouragement do I need to share or experience today?

_____

_____

_____

_____

Prayer
You can turn these experiences into a prayer here or record prayer needs you are lifting to God.

_____

_____

_____

_____

Your Impact Log

Today's Chapter: **Date:**

Truth and Promises:

Father, what are the truths and promises you have for me today?

_____

_____

_____

_____

_____

Adjustments and Assignments:

Holy Spirit, what adjustments and assignments do you have for me today?

_____

_____

_____

_____

Support and Encouragement

What support or encouragement do I need to share or experience today?

_____

_____

_____

_____

Prayer

You can turn these experiences into a prayer here or record prayer needs you are lifting to God.

_____

_____

_____

_____

Your Impact Log

Today's Chapter: **Date:**

Truth and Promises:
Father, what are the truths and promises you have for me today?

_____

_____

_____

_____

Adjustments and Assignments:
Holy Spirit, what adjustments and assignments do you have for me today?

_____

_____

_____

Support and Encouragement
What support or encouragement do I need to share or experience today?

_____

_____

_____

Prayer
You can turn these experiences into a prayer here or record prayer needs you are lifting to God.

_____

_____

_____

Your Impact Log

Today's Chapter: **Date:**

Truth and Promises:
Father, what are the truths and promises you have for me today?

_____

_____

_____

_____

_____

Adjustments and Assignments:
Holy Spirit, what adjustments and assignments do you have for me today?

_____

_____

_____

_____

Support and Encouragement
What support or encouragement do I need to share or experience today?

_____

_____

_____

_____

Prayer
You can turn these experiences into a prayer here or record prayer needs you are lifting to God.

_____

_____

_____

_____

Your Impact Log

Today's Chapter: **Date:**

Truth and Promises:

Father, what are the truths and promises you have for me today?

_____

_____

_____

_____

Adjustments and Assignments:

Holy Spirit, what adjustments and assignments do you have for me today?

_____

_____

_____

Support and Encouragement

What support or encouragement do I need to share or experience today?

_____

_____

_____

Prayer

You can turn these experiences into a prayer here or record prayer needs you are lifting to God.

_____

_____

_____

Your Impact Log

Today's Chapter: **Date:**

Truth and Promises:

Father, what are the truths and promises you have for me today?

_____

_____

_____

_____

_____

Adjustments and Assignments:

Holy Spirit, what adjustments and assignments do you have for me today?

_____

_____

_____

Support and Encouragement

What support or encouragement do I need to share or experience today?

_____

_____

_____

Prayer

You can turn these experiences into a prayer here or record prayer needs you are lifting to God.

_____

_____

_____

_____

Your Impact Log

Today's Chapter: **Date:**

Truth and Promises:

Father, what are the truths and promises you have for me today?

_____

_____

_____

_____

_____

Adjustments and Assignments:

Holy Spirit, what adjustments and assignments do you have for me today?

_____

_____

_____

_____

Support and Encouragement

What support or encouragement do I need to share or experience today?

_____

_____

_____

_____

Prayer

You can turn these experiences into a prayer here or record prayer needs you are lifting to God.

_____

_____

_____

_____

Your Impact Log

Today's Chapter: **Date:**

Truth and Promises:
Father, what are the truths and promises you have for me today?

_____

_____

_____

_____

_____

Adjustments and Assignments:
Holy Spirit, what adjustments and assignments do you have for me today?

_____

_____

_____

Support and Encouragement
What support or encouragement do I need to share or experience today?

_____

_____

_____

Prayer
You can turn these experiences into a prayer here or record prayer needs you are lifting to God.

_____

_____

_____

Your Impact Log

Today's Chapter: **Date:**

Truth and Promises:
Father, what are the truths and promises you have for me today?

_____

_____

_____

_____

_____

Adjustments and Assignments:
Holy Spirit, what adjustments and assignments do you have for me today?

_____

_____

_____

_____

Support and Encouragement
What support or encouragement do I need to share or experience today?

_____

_____

_____

_____

Prayer
You can turn these experiences into a prayer here or record prayer needs you are lifting to God.

_____

_____

_____

_____

Your Impact Log

Today's Chapter: **Date:**

Truth and Promises:
Father, what are the truths and promises you have for me today?

_____

_____

_____

_____

Adjustments and Assignments:
Holy Spirit, what adjustments and assignments do you have for me today?

_____

_____

_____

Support and Encouragement
What support or encouragement do I need to share or experience today?

_____

_____

_____

Prayer
You can turn these experiences into a prayer here or record prayer needs you are lifting to God.

_____

_____

_____

_____

Your Impact Log

Today's Chapter: **Date:**

Truth and Promises:

Father, what are the truths and promises you have for me today?

_____

_____

_____

_____

_____

Adjustments and Assignments:

Holy Spirit, what adjustments and assignments do you have for me today?

_____

_____

_____

Support and Encouragement

What support or encouragement do I need to share or experience today?

_____

_____

_____

Prayer

You can turn these experiences into a prayer here or record prayer needs you are lifting to God.

_____

_____

_____

Your Impact Log

Today's Chapter: **Date:**

Truth and Promises:
Father, what are the truths and promises you have for me today?

_____

_____

_____

_____

_____

Adjustments and Assignments:
Holy Spirit, what adjustments and assignments do you have for me today?

_____

_____

_____

Support and Encouragement
What support or encouragement do I need to share or experience today?

_____

_____

_____

Prayer
You can turn these experiences into a prayer here or record prayer needs you are lifting to God.

_____

_____

_____

Your Impact Log

Today's Chapter: **Date:**

Truth and Promises:
Father, what are the truths and promises you have for me today?

_____

_____

_____

_____

Adjustments and Assignments:
Holy Spirit, what adjustments and assignments do you have for me today?

_____

_____

_____

Support and Encouragement
What support or encouragement do I need to share or experience today?

_____

_____

_____

Prayer
You can turn these experiences into a prayer here or record prayer needs you are lifting to God.

_____

_____

_____

_____

Your Impact Log

Today's Chapter: **Date:**

Truth and Promises:

Father, what are the truths and promises you have for me today?

_____

_____

_____

_____

Adjustments and Assignments:

Holy Spirit, what adjustments and assignments do you have for me today?

_____

_____

_____

Support and Encouragement

What support or encouragement do I need to share or experience today?

_____

_____

_____

Prayer

You can turn these experiences into a prayer here or record prayer needs you are lifting to God.

_____

_____

_____

Your Impact Log

Today's Chapter: **Date:**

Truth and Promises:
Father, what are the truths and promises you have for me today?

_____

_____

_____

_____

Adjustments and Assignments:
Holy Spirit, what adjustments and assignments do you have for me today?

_____

_____

_____

Support and Encouragement
What support or encouragement do I need to share or experience today?

_____

_____

_____

Prayer
You can turn these experiences into a prayer here or record prayer needs you are lifting to God.

_____

_____

_____

Your Impact Log

Today's Chapter: **Date:**

Truth and Promises:
Father, what are the truths and promises you have for me today?

_____

_____

_____

_____

_____

Adjustments and Assignments:
Holy Spirit, what adjustments and assignments do you have for me today?

_____

_____

_____

Support and Encouragement
What support or encouragement do I need to share or experience today?

_____

_____

_____

Prayer
You can turn these experiences into a prayer here or record prayer needs you are lifting to God.

_____

_____

_____

345 My Time Bible Plan
New Testament – 260 Chapters, 52 weeks, 5 Chapters Per Week

Week 1	Acts 11	Romans 15	Week 20
John 1	Acts 12	Romans 16	Philippians 3
John 2	Acts 13		Philippians 4
John 3	Acts 14	Week 14	Colossians 1
John 4		Mark 1	Colossians 2
John 5	Week 8	Mark 2	Colossians 3
	Acts 15	Mark 3	Week 21
Week 2	Acts 16	Mark 4	Colossians 4
John 6	Acts 17	Mark 5	Philemon 1
John 7	Acts 18		1 Corinthians 1
John 8	Acts 19	Week 15	1 Corinthians 2
John 9		Mark 6	1 Corinthians 3
John 10	Week 9	Mark 7	
	Acts 20	Mark 8	Week 22
Week 3	Acts 21	Mark 9	1 Corinthians 4
John 11	Acts 22	Mark 10	1 Corinthians 5
John 12	Acts 23		1 Corinthians 6
John 13	Acts 24	Week 16	1 Corinthians 7
John 14		Mark 11	1 Corinthians 8
John 15	Week 10	Mark 12	
	Acts 25	Mark 13	Week 23
Week 4	Acts 26	Mark 14	1 Corinthians 9
John 16	Acts 27	Mark 15	1 Corinthians 10
John 17	Acts 28		1 Corinthians 11
John 18	Romans 1	Week 17	1 Corinthians 12
John 19		Mark 16	1 Corinthians 13
John 20	Week 11	Galatians 1	
	Romans 2	Galatians 2	Week 24
Week 5	Romans 3	Galatians 3	1 Corinthians 14
John 21	Romans 4	Galatians 4	1 Corinthians 15
Acts 1	Romans 5		1 Corinthians 16
Acts 2	Romans 6	Week 18	2 Corinthians 1
Acts 3		Galatians 5	2 Corinthians 2
Acts 4	Week 12	Galatians 6	
	Romans 7	Ephesians 1	Week 25
Week 6	Romans 8	Ephesians 2	2 Corinthians 3
Acts 5	Romans 9	Ephesians 3	2 Corinthians 4
Acts 6	Romans 10		2 Corinthians 5
Acts 7	Romans 11	Week 19	2 Corinthians 6
Acts 8		Ephesians 4	2 Corinthians 7
Acts 9	Week 13	Ephesians 5	
	Romans 12	Ephesians 6	Week 26
Week 7	Romans 13	Philippians 1	2 Corinthians 8
Acts 10	Romans 14	Philippians 2	2 Corinthians 9

Luke 19

Multiplying Impact Teams

Would you consider starting a team (small group) where people can share from the three essential experiences with God? All it takes is a time, place, and followers of Christ engaged in this process. The goal of a group like this is not a presentation or teaching but sharing what the Lord has revealed through our time with Him.

The purpose of an Impact Team is two-fold:

1. Giving people an opportunity to share from the three experiences of their daily Impact Journey.
2. Making an Impact in the community together by meeting a need or healing a hurt (seeking team assignments from the Holy Spirit) shining with the love of Jesus and sharing Christ when people are open (1 Peter 3:15, 18).

When you meet...

There are three things to do and three things to avoid.

Do:

1. Discuss truth and promises that God highlighted to each individual in the previous week.
2. Share any adjustments or assignments given by the Holy Spirit to individuals in the previous week.
3. Support and encourage one another (prayers and words of affirmation).

Avoid:

1. Trying to fix one another. That is the role of the Holy Spirit. He doesn't need helpers.
2. Gossip. Talking about other people's issues is not ok. We should focus on our own thoughts and feelings.
3. Becoming an 'agreement group' and not taking Christ to the community.

A Tri-Personal Prayer
Father, Son, and Holy Spirit

Father, thank you for taking action to restore my relationship with you, even though you did nothing to cause the problem. You are such a good Father (Luke 15:11-32). Thank you for being available to me at all times (Hebrews 4:16). Thank you for welcoming me, listening, and forgiving me (Isaiah 1:18). You love me completely because of Jesus (John 17:23). Thank you for accepting me through Jesus, forgiving my sins, and granting me the righteous standing of Christ because of Your amazing grace! (2 Corinthians 5:21)

My Lord Jesus, Savior, Friend. Thank you for saving my soul and restoring my relationship with God my Father. Thank you for living the life I should have lived and dying in my place for my sins. Thank you for conquering death to prove your power to save all who call upon your name (Romans 10:13). I trust you Jesus as my Savior and Lord. Help me to have your mindset and motives in all my decisions. (1 John 1:9, Philippians 2:5-11). Let your love and wisdom guide my actions and reactions this day.

Spirit of God, thank you for coming into my life. Fill me and drive out the impulses and attitudes from my life that do not reflect the character of Jesus (2 Peter 1:4). Fill my heart with the love of God (Romans 5:5). You are my union with the Father and the Son. You are the Spirit of truth in me, the life of God in me, my Counselor, Comforter, Strength, and Guide. Lead me deeper into the love of Jesus Christ (Ephesians 3:18). Bring opportunities for me to share Christ and wisdom to seize them well. Let my speech be seasoned with grace and truth. Bring encouragement into our lives today. Raise up a full canopy of prayer, encouragement, and provision over us all (John 16:13-15).

Spiritual Warfare/Protection Prayer
Knowing that followers of Christ have no enemies with flesh and blood enemies, I pray now, in the name and authority of Jesus Christ alone, against any foul or unclean spirit that attempts to come against us. I pray against any work of the enemy or ungodly schemes within people, that they would be repelled by the power of Jesus Christ and bound away from us in His good name. And in Jesus' worthy name, I summon holy angel warriors to camp around us, defend us from every attack, and destroy the works of the enemy towards us. I pray for angelic protection over our families, our household, and those we reach out to, share Christ with, and invite to be a part of the family of God (Ephesians 6:10-11).
Thank you Father God for hearing my prayer. Let be mindful of You throughout this day. Let me be sensitive to the adjustments and assignments the Holy Spirit has for me. Let whatever I do in word or deed, be done in the name of Jesus and to Your glory.
In Jesus' good name I pray,
Amen

"And whatever you do or say, do it as a representative of the Lord Jesus, giving thanks through him to God the Father."
Colossians 3:17

The Lord bless you,
and keep you,
make His face shine upon you,
and be gracious to you,
the Lord turn His face towards you,
and give you peace.

Timothy Moore
Executive Director
Impact Multiplied